Shark Park

Chris McTrustry

Illustrated by Ned Culic

ETA Cuisenaire

ETA Cuisenaire
800-445-5985 www.etacuisenaire.com

Shark Park

ISBN 978-0740-61207-7
ETA 620071

ETA/Cuisenaire • Vernon Hills, IL 60061-1862
800-445-5985 • www.etacuisenaire.com

Published by ETA/Cuisenaire® under license from
Pearson Australia
(a division of Pearson Australia Group Pty Ltd)

Text by Chris McTrustry
Edited by Philip Bryan
Designed by Caz Brown
Illustrated by Ned Culic

Printed in China (SWTC/04)

10 11 12 13 10 9 8 7 6 5 4

Contents

CHAPTER 1

The Shark-Stopping Backpack

"Come on, Anita," urged Sam. He pointed ahead of them at the shipwreck. "Once we're out of the water, the shark won't be able to hurt us."

Anita was about to cry. "I can't keep up, Sam," she whispered. "The shark is going to get us. I know it!" She looked over her shoulder at the deep blue water. It was so still and dark—and dangerous.

"You can't give up now!" said Sam, heroically. He shifted his backpack and reached out for Anita. "Here, take my hand."

Then a swishing sound grew louder. Ripples of water washed around them.

"Oh no!" said Sam. He grabbed Anita by the arm and dragged her toward him. He smiled nervously. "Our 'friend' is back ..."

Suddenly, the water started to bubble. Then a fin broke the surface. It cut through the water like a hot knife into butter, heading straight for Sam and Anita.

Anita screamed.

Sam took the backpack from his shoulder and held it in front of him. "We have one chance," he said grimly.

Then the shark broke the surface of the water. It opened its mouth, showing a set of dagger-sharp teeth.

Anita **screamed** again.

The shark was close to Sam and Anita when Sam made his move. He thrust his backpack at the shark with a mighty heave. The pack lodged in the shark's mouth, it slowed, and—

—and then someone laughed.

"CUT!" screamed Thomas Larkin, the director of *Bite*. "Stop the camera!" He pushed out of his chair and stomped down to the water's edge. "Who was that? Who *laughed*?"

A boy raised his hand and smiled sheepishly. He was crouching in a rubber dinghy anchored in the shallow water.

Mr. Larkin sighed. "Jake!" he said. "I should have guessed it was *you*."

"Sorry, Mr. Larkin," said the boy. "But there is no way a backpack would stop a shark attack."

Thomas Larkin bit down hard on his bottom lip. "Dr. Edwards!" he screamed, looking around the set.

Doctor Linda Edwards climbed out of the water. She was a tall woman, wearing a blue wetsuit. She walked over to the director.

"Yes, Mr. Larkin," she said. "You bellowed?"

"Ah, Dr. Edwards," Mr. Larkin smiled. "Another of your jokes. Very funny—I don't think! Once again, we have to stop filming because of your son."

Jake Edwards slipped off the rubber dinghy and waded ashore.

"You couldn't stop a shark by putting a backpack into its mouth. **NO WAY!**" he said. "Tell him, Mom."

Dr. Edwards sighed. "He's right, Mr. Larkin."

"So what?" said Mr. Larkin. "Who cares? I am making a movie. A movie has to *entertain*. Dr. Edwards, you are here to give expert advice—when *I* ask for it." He pointed at Jake. "Your son is not meant to be here at all. And he is definitely *not* an expert."

"I know more about sharks than you do," said Jake.

Dr. Edwards gestured to Jake. "We'll wait in our trailer, Mr. Larkin," she said. "If you need me, just call. Come on, Jake."

"Thank you, Dr. Edwards." Mr. Larkin turned to his actors and crew. He clapped his hands. "Okay, people, let's set up this scene again. Maybe without any more interruptions we'll finish before dark!"

Chapter 2

A One-Legged Shark Expert

"Why won't Larkin listen to you?" asked Jake. "There can't be more than three or four people in the whole world who know more about sharks than you."

Jake's mom stopped typing and looked up from her laptop computer. She smiled. "That's nice of you to say so, Jake."

Dr. Edwards rapped her knuckles hard against her left leg. There was a hollow-sounding "**THOCK**." "But some people don't believe you're such a shark expert if a shark has taken one of your legs." She returned to her typing.

"Then they're stupid," said Jake. He pushed up onto an elbow and watched his mom working. "What are you writing?

An advance review of Larkin's movie masterpiece?"

"Actually, I'm applying for a lecturing job in a university," said Dr. Edwards. "It's time I got a permanent job."

"Cool!" said Jake. "We'll have a real home. No more trailers and hotel rooms."

Dr. Edwards stopped typing. She frowned at her son. "I thought you liked life on the road," she said.

Jake shrugged. "It's all right for a little while. But a real home—where you don't have to walk fifty yards to take a shower—would be **MEGA COOL!**"

For the next few days, Jake stayed away from the movie set and concentrated on his schoolwork.

"It's not fair," he told his mom one night over dinner. "Thanks to computers and e-mail, there is definitely no escaping homework."

"Thanks for reminding me," said his mom. "While I wash the dishes, you can log on and see if you have any homework to do."

Jake groaned. "Me and my **BIG** mouth," he said. "I hate computers."

He dumped his dinner plate in the kitchen's tiny sink and shuffled over to his mom's desk. Jake booted up the laptop and logged on to the Internet. He scanned the list of new mail and groaned.

"Surprise, surprise," he said. "Mr. Jones has sent me two files of homework."

"Lucky you," chuckled Dr. Edwards.

"There's mail for you, too," said Jake. "From a Mr. Charles Lamb."

Jake looked up and frowned. "He's from a place called Shark Park."

Helipad
Reception
White Pointer "Jaws"
Walking Tunnel
Access Hatch
Shark-Holding Pen
Information Hut
Arcade Island
Underground Viewing Area
Tiger Shark
Bull Shark
SHARK PARK

CHAPTER 3

Welcome to Shark Park

The helicopter swooped low over the island. From his window seat, Jake could see the outer edges of Shark Park. A network of artificial canals criss-crossed the island, linking shark displays and fairground rides. As the helicopter cut its way inland, Jake realized that Shark Park occupied most of the island.

"Look, Mom! There's a Ferris wheel!" gasped Jake. "And it's **HUGE!**"

Dr. Edwards leaned across to gaze out of the window. She shook her head.

"Mr. Lamb told me he was serious about sharks," she sighed. "But to me, Shark Park looks like nothing more than an amusement park."

"Don't be too hasty, Mom," said Jake. "Let's see what Mr. Lamb has to say before we make any judgments."

His mom smiled. "Listen to you," she said. "You sound very grown up."

"Exactly," grinned Jake. "I want to show everyone—including Mr. Lamb—that I'm not some **SILLY** kid." He nodded at the island stretched out below them. "And that looks like a great place to live and work."

"To live *and* work?" asked Dr. Edwards.

"Yeah," said Jake. "Think of all the research you could do!"

"I see," said Dr. Edwards. "And I guess you could find a part-time job to keep yourself busy."

"You bet I could!" said Jake, enthusiastically. "And did you see the surf? Did you see those waves breaking on the beach?"

"Just remember, we're here to make sure this park is safe for sharks—and for humans," said his mom. "My report will decide whether Shark Park is allowed to open to the public."

The helicopter dropped in altitude as it neared the center of the island. A cluster of buildings sat in a large clearing. The clearing was ringed by palm trees and sliced in half by a wide, crystal-clear stream. The buildings were designed to look like island huts. Very **BIG** island huts. The helicopter landed at the rear of the "huts."

A tall, thin man was waiting near the landing pad. He was dressed completely in white.

"Greetings, visitors," he said, as he helped Jake and his mom from the helicopter. "I'm Charles Lamb. Welcome to Shark Park."

"Cool," said Jake.

Mr. Lamb smiled. "Cool? Yes, indeedy-do! Cool!"

Jake's mom shook Mr. Lamb's hand. "I'm Dr. Linda Edwards," she said. "And this is Jake."

"The pleasure is all mine," said Mr. Lamb, grinning. "I'll arrange for your bags to be taken to your rooms. But first, let me tell you about Shark Park."

Jake and his mom followed Mr. Lamb toward a large hut. "Shark Park is to be a haven for sharks," said Mr. Lamb. "Sharks are our misunderstood friends. And at the same time, Shark Park is to be an entertaining place. We have managed to get the balance between entertainment and education just right."

Mr. Lamb looked up at the sky. "The day is young," he said. "I thought we'd take a tour of the park." He pointed between the two largest huts. "The tour starts down there, behind Reception. I'll get my hat and then we can start."

Ten minutes later, Jake and his mom were seated at the outdoor cafe behind Reception. They were sipping cool drinks.

"This is the LIFE," sighed Jake, raising his glass in a toast.

Dr. Edwards smiled. "It certainly is very relaxing." She nodded up at a gathering bank of gray clouds. "But I think we're in for some nasty weather."

"No way," said Jake. "We'll probably just get a tropical shower. It will be just enough to cool the place down."

"Good afternoon, honored guests," said a voice from behind them. A woman dressed in blue smiled at Jake and his mom. "I'm Mr. Lamb's personal assistant. My name's Angela." She handed Dr. Edwards an information folder about Shark Park. "Mr. Lamb will join you soon."

Suddenly, a whirling sound grew louder and louder. A **LARGE** shadow flashed over the heads of Jake and his mom.

"Hey!" exclaimed Jake. "There goes our ride!"

Angela smiled. "The helicopter will return in two days. Mr. Lamb has given the staff a two-day holiday."

"So it's just the four of us on the island?" asked Dr. Edwards.

"Five," said Angela. "Mr. Lamb's daughter, Eliza, has stayed on the island." She smiled again. "If you need anything, please call me." Angela gave a small bow, then left.

"What do you think, Mom?" asked Jake. "Do you think Mr. Lamb knows much about sharks?"

His mom looked up from reading the folder and smiled. "I think he knows a lot about making money from sharks. But as for the sharks themselves? No, I don't think he knows a lot. But let's wait for the tour. Perhaps he'll surprise us."

Jake nodded. It would be very interesting to find out if Shark Park was the shark reserve that Mr. Lamb claimed it to be.

CHAPTER 4

Nature in the Raw

Charles Lamb wore a Panama hat. It was white, of course, and it had a hatband studded with shark's teeth.

"It's for the tourists," he chuckled, when Jake protested about the shark's teeth. "They see sharks as **BIG, SCARY MONSTERS**. The general public aren't as educated as you and I, Jake."

Dr. Edwards tapped the information folder. "Do you really have 40 different species of shark in the park?"

Mr. Lamb smiled and nodded. "Yes, indeedy-do! And we're working on getting more." He turned to Jake.

"And we have the three big boys: the white pointer, the tiger shark, and the bull shark."

"Very impressive," said Dr. Edwards.

"Our transport is impressive, too," said Mr. Lamb. He pointed at a long boat. From a distance it looked like a gray canoe, but a closer look showed a modern, metal, engine-driven boat. "It's automatic. It's run completely by computer. Amazing things, computers. The boat is on submerged rails and driven along by magnets. It's all very scientific. We just sit back and enjoy the ride."

They climbed into the canoe. Mr. Lamb took a seat at the front, while Jake and his mom settled in seats at the rear.

Jake picked up the discarded Shark Park folder. He rested it on his mom's laptop computer and flicked through it. Suddenly, he had the feeling he was being watched. He looked up. A girl was looking at him and smiling.

"Hi," she said, as she climbed into the canoe.

"Hi," said Jake. "You must be Eliza."

"That's right," said the girl. "And you must be Jake." Eliza was around Jake's age. Her bleached hair and tanned skin were clearly the result of a life spent in the tropics. "Dad said I could come on the tour, too."

Jake frowned. "Haven't you been around the park yet?"

Eliza shook her head. "Not yet. Dad's almost finished work on it. Some of the exhibits only arrived last week. Some still haven't arrived..."

"Thank you, Eliza," said Mr. Lamb, curtly. "I'll be the one leading the tour."

Eliza bowed her head. "Sorry, Dad."

Mr. Lamb stood at the front of the canoe and smiled. "Everything is ready," he said. "Prepare to be amazed! Prepare to be scared! Prepare to learn!"

Mr. Lamb sat at the front of the canoe. He pushed a button on a remote control and the canoe moved forward. The "river" twisted this way and that and soon they were in a thick "jungle." Up ahead, to the left, Jake could see a large pool.

Then, suddenly, the "river" dipped down and they roller-coasted under the ground. They plunged down a dark tunnel and emerged in a brightly lit cavern. The "river" flowed through the cavern. On one side of the cavern was thick glass, giving a clear view of the pool Jake had seen.

"It's like a huge aquarium," gasped Jake.

"Yes, indeedy-do!" said Mr. Lamb. He pointed at the pool. "And look over here: One of my guests is coming to say 'hi.'"

A dark, blurred shape powered through the water toward the pool's porthole.

"WHOA!" gasped Jake. "That's a WHITE POINTER!"

Dr. Edwards leaned forward, peering at the shark. "It must be four yards long," she said softly.

"Four and a half yards, to be precise," Mr. Lamb chuckled. "We call him Jaws. Isn't he a beauty?"

"What do you feed him?" asked Dr. Edwards.

Mr. Lamb just smiled."Watch and find out ..." he said.

Jaws swept smoothly along the edge of the glass a couple of times. He looked graceful, powerful. Suddenly, there was a splashing near the pool's surface. Jaws slowed his swimming and focused on the splashing.

"What is that?" asked Dr. Edwards. She stared at Mr. Lamb. "Is that someone in a boat?"

Mr Lamb nodded. "It's dinnertime," he said.

Suddenly, a deep red mist spread through the water. "Angela is tossing in chunks of fresh meat," Mr. Lamb explained. "After all, a giant like Jaws can't live on fish flakes."

A large lump of meat sank near the aquarium porthole. The shark zeroed in on it and made its move.

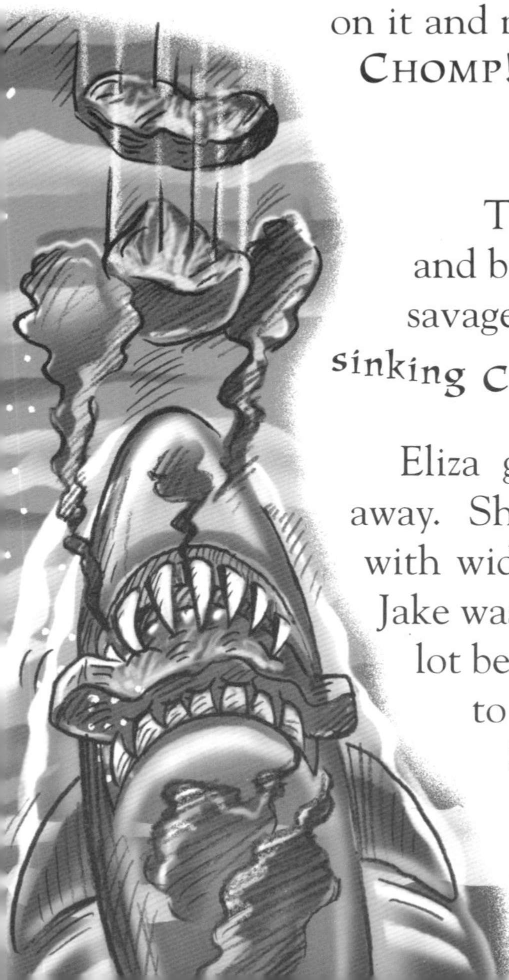

CHOMP!

CHOMP!

CHOMP!

The water swirled and bubbled as the shark savagely ripped into the sinking CHUNKS of meat.

Eliza gasped and turned away. She looked at Jake with wide, frightened eyes. Jake wasn't feeling a whole lot better, but he nodded to Eliza and smiled. She smiled weakly, then put her face in her hands.

Soon, the meat was devoured and the water became still. Without a glance at its audience, Jaws swam away.

"Why was the attack so frenzied?" asked Dr. Edwards.

Mr. Lamb shrugged. "I'm not sure. Maybe Jaws missed breakfast this morning …"

"Dinner, too, I'd say," muttered Jake.

Mr. Lamb smiled and said nothing.

Eliza slowly lifted her head. "Is it over yet?"

"Yes, it's over," said Dr. Edwards.

The canoe started moving forward.

"I make no apologies," said Mr. Lamb. "This is nature in the raw. And if sharks are brutal …" He shrugged. "Then brutal is what the public gets."

The canoe started heading upwards.

"But not all sharks are brutal," protested Jake. "Out of 350 species, only about 30 species have been known to attack people."

Mr. Lamb sighed. "I know that, Jake; you know that, your mom knows that." He grinned. "But the public doesn't. And this is what they want."

Chapter 5

All Sharks and No Play

They emerged from the tunnel and entered a large saltwater lake. The blue sky had faded to a dull grey. Thick clouds scudded across the sky, looming low over the tops of the palm trees.

"What do you think of my island?" asked Mr. Lamb. He was pointing at an island in the middle of the lake. "We flooded this section of the island to make a lake, then added a special fun island. We call it Arcade Island."

Mr. Lamb smiled. "After all, **ALL SHARKS** and **NO PLAY** makes little kiddies **VERY** naughty."

"Perhaps we could skip Arcade Island," said Dr. Edwards.

"Oh, Mom," said Jake. "Can't we check out the rides?"

"No, Jake," said his mom, firmly. She turned to Mr. Lamb. "I read about shark-holding pens in the folder you gave me. I'd like to see those—and any other enclosures—before the rain starts."

Mr. Lamb shook his head. "Unfortunately, the canoe is on a pre-set computer program. We can't change our course. We are on the Tour Course—and on the Tour Course we must stay."

The canoe chugged across the lake. Jake let his hand brush across the lake's surface. He leaned over the side of the canoe, peering into the water. Dark figures darted about.

"What's in here?" asked Jake.

"Sharks, of course!" said Mr. Lamb.

"What?" said Jake. He quickly withdrew his hand.

"They're not dangerous sharks," Eliza said. "They all get along famously."

Sure, thought Jake. As long as they're fed regularly …

"I have basking sharks in there. Some mako sharks, too," said Mr. Lamb. "It was quite difficult buying all these fish."

"Fish?" spluttered Jake. "They're not *fish*, they're SHARKS…"

"This lake has viewing ports," said Mr. Lamb, talking over Jake, "just like the ones you saw earlier. There are walking tunnels on either side of the lake for those who don't like boat travel."

Jake looked from one edge of the lake to the other. "That's some walk," he said.

"We have motorized carts for those who need assistance," said Mr. Lamb.

A sudden CRACK of thunder made everyone look up at the sky.

"There's a storm coming," said Dr. Edwards. "Perhaps we should head back to Reception."

"And we shall, Doctor. Unfortunately, we must follow the pre-set course," said Mr. Lamb.

Large drops of rain bounced off the lake. Jake turned to his mom. "Do you believe this nonsense about not being able to change course?" he whispered.

She shook her head. "No."

"And why doesn't he want you to see the holding pens?"

"You noticed that, too?" said his mom. "I don't know why. But I'll check it out tomorrow."

Tigers and Bulls

There was another thunderclap, closer this time.

The canoe chugged on as they passed Arcade Island. The light turned a dull gray and drizzle started to fall. Suddenly, the lights on the Ferris wheel twinkled into life. Lights on the other rides came to life, too. The yellow glow of the lights against the darkening sky made Arcade Island look **creepy**.

Maybe it was best to keep on going, thought Jake. The sooner they were back at Reception and out of the rain, the better.

"The holding pens are over there," said Mr. Lamb. He pointed to the left shore of the lake. Jake turned away from

Arcade Island and squinted through the sheets of rain. He could just see the dim outline of a fence.

"We corral the sharks there and guide them to their pools," said Mr. Lamb. "The holding pens are off-limits to the public."

"How do you *guide* a shark?" wondered Jake.

"I definitely want to see the holding pens," said Jake's mom. She pulled her jacket tight across her shoulders. "But I think tomorrow would be a better time."

"I couldn't agree more," said Mr. Lamb. The canoe headed further across the lake. "We'll soon be at Shark Park's second-biggest attraction."

"Is it a whale shark?" asked Jake.

Mr. Lamb shook his head. "Unfortunately, no. But a whale shark is on my shopping list."

Lightning ripped along the tops of the palm trees. Then another crack of thunder rolled out of the sky. A howling wind whipped across the water, chopping its surface.

"This is ridiculous," said Dr. Edwards. She leaned toward Mr. Lamb. "Would you conduct a public tour in weather like this?"

"Of course not!" said Mr. Lamb. "It would be too dangerous."

"Then what are we doing out here?" asked Jake.

"Maybe we should head back, Dad," said Eliza.

"We are heading back, Eliza," grunted Mr. Lamb. "The rain is only light. And I want to show Dr. Edwards the pools where we keep the tiger and bull sharks."

"I have Jaws at the start of the tour,"

said Mr. Lamb, "and these BRUTES at the end. The tour starts with a bang and finishes with a—"

KA-RACK!

A fierce crack of thunder crashed across the sky. The rain became heavier, lashing down and soaking everyone.

"I know the tour hasn't been as good as it could be," said Mr. Lamb. "But I wanted you to see the whole tour in one outing."

"My report won't be based just on the tour," said Jake's mom. "How you care for the sharks will also be looked at. And at the moment, I haven't—"

"Yes, yes, I know!" snapped Mr. Lamb. He tugged down the brim of his hat. A waterfall of water splashed over him.

Jake laughed out loud. He couldn't help himself.

Ahead of the canoe, Mr. Lamb's artificial lake narrowed into a thin "river."

"The tiger shark pool is ahead of us." Mr. Lamb pointed to a large metal gate painted in tiger stripes.

"There are two gates," Mr. Lamb went on. "They are both computer-operated. The inner gate opens and the shark enters. That gate closes, then the outer gate opens. The same system operates on the other side of the pool for the bull sharks."

Mr. Lamb smiled at Dr. Edwards. "We have **TIGHT** safety and security at Shark Park," he said.

The sky lit up with a flash of lightning, just as the river dipped and the canoe headed underground again.

CHAPTER 7

Sharks Are Not Performing Seals

"It's the same setup as with Jaws," said Mr. Lamb. "But this time, the two pools form a semicircle. We view the tiger sharks from this side, then swing around to view the bull sharks. Then we head home—"

Suddenly the lights in the tunnel flickered. They went **OFF**, came back **ON**, then went **OFF** again. It was completely dark.

The canoe groaned, then ground to a halt. It wasn't going anywhere without power.

"Terrific," muttered Jake.

"There's no cause for alarm," said Mr. Lamb. He laughed nervously and punched a button on the remote control. A small set of headlights burst into life.

"Do you have a backup power source?" asked Dr. Edwards.

"Of course, of course," said Mr. Lamb.

"A reserve generator should kick in automatically," said Eliza.

"It must need a big kick," said Jake.

Eliza giggled. "The computer system is very complicated. But the power source isn't."

"You seem to know a lot about it, Eliza," said Dr. Edwards.

"I helped test some of the Park's power systems," said Eliza.

Jake pointed at the tiger shark pool. "HUH," he said, disappointed. "No one's home."

"We can't expect Angela to come way out here to tempt the sharks to show themselves," said his mom.

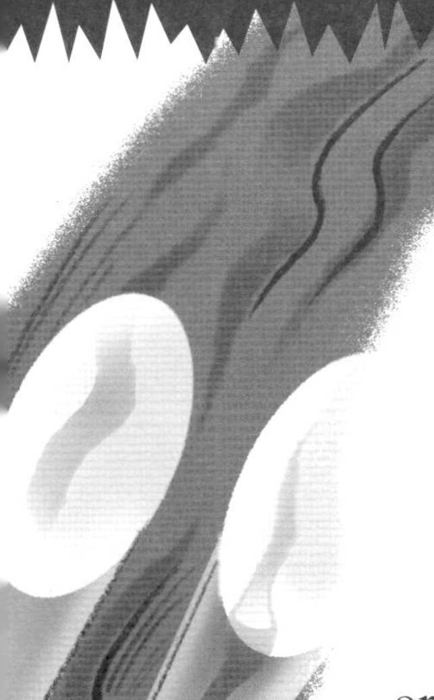

"I agree with Jake," said Mr. Lamb. "Those **BRUTES** should be swimming by."

"They're not performing seals, Mr. Lamb," said Dr. Edwards.

Mr. Lamb said nothing.

The overhead lights flickered **ON** and **OFF**. The canoe jerked forward, then all the lights came on.

"Hooray!" cheered Jake and Eliza. They were on the move again.

The bull sharks also failed to appear as the canoe passed by. The canoe turned to the right and started up the tunnel.

Mr. Lamb stood in the front of the canoe facing Jake and his mom. "Our tour is complete," he said cheerfully.

"Hooray," muttered Jake. "Now we can all get wet …"

The canoe moved smoothly out of the tunnel. Out on the lake, the rain continued to pour down.

"Is there somewhere we can get shelter?" shouted Dr. Edwards.

She had to shout to be heard over the storm. The thunder **BOOMED** and lightning **LIT UP** the sky, flashing across the gray clouds. The rain **RAT-A-TATTED** on the metal canoe.

Mr. Lamb nodded. "There are a number of smaller attractions along the way back to Reception," he said, screwing up his face. "Scientific nonsense. History."

"The serious stuff, you mean," said Jake.

"It might be serious to you, Jake. But to the average ticket-buying member of the public, it's boring."

"Boring?" asked Jake. "No way. If you read a quarter of what Mom has written about sharks—"

"Jake!" said his mom. "This isn't the time or the place to discuss these matters."

"Isn't anyone else getting wet?" asked Eliza. She huddled in her seat.

"We'll get shelter at the Information Hut," said Mr. Lamb. "We can sit out the storm there."

WHAM! Suddenly, the canoe rocked violently sideways.

"What was that?" asked Mr. Lamb.

Jake glared at Mr. Lamb. "Don't *you* know what that was?"

Eliza screamed. "L-l-look!" she stammered. She was pointing at the fence around the bull shark pool.

"The gates are open!" said Jake.

"That's impossible!" said Mr. Lamb.

"There must have been a lightning strike," said Dr. Edwards.

"That would explain the power failure," gasped Eliza. "Lightning would short out the entire system. The whole system must have failed."

WHAM! The canoe was rocked sideways again.

"What *is* that?" asked Jake. "The canoe isn't coming off the rails, is it?"

"It's not the canoe," said his mom. "Look over there." Two shark fins were cutting through the water toward the canoe. She turned to Mr. Lamb. "Your guests are OUT," she said. "And they're **HUNGRY**."

Shark Attack!

"Can this canoe go any faster?" asked Jake.

Mr. Lamb nodded grimly. "I can crank it up a little."

"Then do it!" shouted Jake.

Mr. Lamb looked from Jake to Jake's mom, then to Eliza. "If we go too fast, the canoe will leave the rails," he yelled.

Dr. Edwards pointed at the circling sharks. "And if we go too slow, the sharks will tip the canoe over." Her eyes narrowed. "Did you forget to feed these sharks as well?"

Mr. Lamb nodded. "I didn't think they'd be hungry…" He picked up the remote. "I'll bump the speed up a little. We'll make a run for the Information Hut."

The canoe rattled as the speed was increased. The rain continued to fall—but no one was worried about rain anymore.

"I hope Jaws isn't out of his cage," said Jake.

"Luckily, he's been fed," said his mom.

The Information Hut was fifty yards ahead. Jake could just see it through the sheets of rain. Then, suddenly, **WHAM**—the canoe lurched violently to the right.

"**AAAARGH!**" screamed Eliza. She almost fell out of the canoe. Dr. Edwards swiveled around and caught Eliza by the arm. Together, Jake and his mom dragged Eliza back into the canoe.

Dr. Edwards was angry. "This whole tour has been nothing but a DISASTER!" She turned to Mr. Lamb. "Oh, no!" she gasped.

Mr. Lamb lay slumped in the front of the boat, unconscious.

"**DAD!**" screamed Eliza.

Eliza and Dr. Edwards tried to lift Mr. Lamb, but he was too heavy. "You'll have to help us, Jake," said his mom.

"Here I come," said Jake. He hurried to the front of the canoe.

Together, Eliza, Jake, and his mom eased Mr. Lamb to a sitting position.

Mr. Lamb was slowly waking up. "Th-thank you," he gasped. He mopped a cut on his forehead with his handkerchief.

"Are you okay?" asked Dr. Edwards. "That's a nasty cut. We need to get you back to Reception."

Mr. Lamb gave a crooked grin. "I'm afraid I won't be able to move too fast." He winced. "I've twisted my ankle."

Jake took charge as the canoe bumped into the dock. "Okay," he said, "everyone out." He snatched up the laptop computer, climbed onto the dock, then helped get Mr. Lamb into the Information Hut.

CHAPTER 9

Jake Takes Charge

"I've got a plan," said Jake, as they sheltered in the Information Hut. "We head down to the walking tunnels and get a motorized cart. Then we drive back along the tunnels to Reception. We'll be safe and dry in fifteen minutes."

"I can't walk too far," said Mr. Lamb.

"You won't have to walk far if we follow Jake's plan," said Eliza.

With Jake and Eliza supporting Mr. Lamb, they edged their way down the corridor to the walking tunnel.

Dr. Edwards hurried down the tunnel after them. She eased herself under Mr. Lamb's arm and helped to support him. "The telephone is still dead," she said.

"Too bad," said Jake. "If we could call Angela, she could have met us halfway with a medical kit."

"I'll be fine," said Mr. Lamb. "But the sooner we find a cart, the happier I'll be."

"Leave that to me," said Jake. He made sure Eliza and his mom had a firm hold on Mr. Lamb. Then he ran ahead, searching for motorized carts.

But five minutes later, Jake returned—on foot. "I couldn't find any carts," he said.

Mr. Lamb groaned. "All the carts must be at Reception." He slumped against a wall. "Leave me here. You three head back to Reception. Send Angela to fetch me."

"No!" said Eliza. "You're coming, too."

"I agree with Eliza," said Dr. Edwards. "If the system has failed, who knows what will happen next."

They entered the tunnel and made their way slowly toward Reception. But they had gone less than 200 yards when all the lights went out. The tunnel was filled with thick, cold, black darkness.

"Don't panic!" said Mr. Lamb.

"Who stands in the **DARK** and doesn't panic?" asked Jake.

Jake waved his hand in front of his face. He felt the breeze, but he couldn't see his hand. The only sound was the rapid breathing of the four adventurers.

"When will the lights come back on?" asked Jake.

Mr. Lamb cleared his throat. "When the reserve generator kicks in, Jake," he said. "It will probably happen soon."

"And if the lights don't come back on?" asked Dr. Edwards. "What happens then?"

Mr. Lamb gasped. "Of course! There's a service shed in this tunnel. There will be flashlights or lanterns there."

"Which way is it?" asked Dr. Edwards.

"It's back by the tunnel entrance," said Mr. Lamb.

"Let's go!" said Jake.

"Wait!" said his mom. "Jake and Eliza, don't go wandering off. We don't want anyone getting lost."

"But we can't just *stand* here," said Eliza.

"Hang on!" said Jake. He was fumbling with something. There was a **ZIP**, then a **CLICK**, then a motor started to **WHIR**. The silver screen of the laptop slowly glowed into life.

"Light!" said Eliza. "Excellent, Jake!"

"Yes," said Mr. Lamb, "well done, Jake."

Using the glow from the laptop's screen as a light, they edged their way back along the tunnel to the service shed. After a short search, they found flashlights and miners' hats with battery-powered lanterns.

"It's best to be prepared," said Mr. Lamb.

"When *will* the reserve generator kick in?" asked Dr. Edwards.

Mr. Lamb shrugged. "As I said before: It should come on soon, I suppose."

Which could be *never*, thought Jake.

"But the reserve generator was lighting the tunnel," said Eliza. "It had to be. The main system failed when we were in the tiger and bull tunnel. The reserve generator started, but I think it's failed, too."

Eliza turned to Jake and his mom. "I helped the workers sometimes, so I know a bit about the power source." She put her hands on her hips. "We need to get back to the main compound and re-boot the system."

"Well, what are we waiting for?" asked Jake. He edged past Eliza and strode along the tunnel. Eliza hurried after him.

Jake shone his flashlight beam onto the roof of the tunnel. It was smooth and perfectly round, like a mole tunnel. He was about to comment on the tunnel's shape when he heard something.

Eliza heard it, too. She turned to Jake. "What's that noise?" she asked.

"I don't know," shrugged Jake. "It sounds like a toilet flushing."

"Oh, no!" gasped Mr. Lamb. He spun Jake and Eliza around and pointed back toward the service shed. "The tunnels are flooding! **RUN!**"

Crash! Splash!

They ran back down the tunnel toward the shed. Water was lapping at their feet.

"Shut the door!" shouted Mr. Lamb when they were in the shed.

"That won't keep out all that water," said Dr. Edwards.

"Any obstacle will help," said Mr. Lamb. He shone his flashlight at a barred security door. "We go through here."

Jake pushed the door open and shone his flashlight inside. A long, narrow corridor led to a ladder.

"That ladder leads up to an access hatch," said Mr. Lamb. "If we get through there, we're safe from water and sharks!"

"So let's go!" exclaimed Jake.

A rumbling noise grew **louder** and **louder**. A wall of water was rushing down the corridor behind them.

With a mighty **CRASH,** the water bulldozed into the service shed and flowed into the corridor. It filled quickly, rising to their knees.

"Eliza, you go up first," said Mr. Lamb. "You'll have to push hard to shift the access hatch cover."

Eliza scrambled up the ladder. With a mighty heave, she slid away the hatch cover and climbed through.

"Quick, Jake, you're next!" said Dr. Edwards.

"No," said Jake. "You have to go next, Mom."

"Is this because you want to be a hero, Jake?" asked his mom, glaring at him. "If it is—"

"It's not!" yelled Jake. "You're the only one who can haul Mr. Lamb up the ladder!"

Jake's mom looked from Jake to Mr. Lamb. Water was flooding into the corridor.

"Alright," she said. "Mr. Lamb and I will go next. But you'd better be right behind us."

"I will," said Jake.

Eliza called down from the access hatch. "What's going on? HURRY UP!"

Jake and his mom helped Mr. Lamb onto the second rung of the ladder. Dr. Edwards started up the ladder slowly, dragging Mr. Lamb behind her.

Jake watched them climb the ladder. He shivered. The water had risen up to his waist. Suddenly, he heard a splashing noise. He looked along the corridor. There was a flash of gray and white; then a FIN broke the surface.

"Mom!"

Jake's mom twisted around on the ladder. She saw the shark's fin cutting through the water—it was heading straight for Jake.

"Get on the ladder, Jake!" she shouted. "Get on **NOW!**"

But there was no room for Jake on the ladder. Mr. Lamb had only climbed three rungs. Jake would not be able to climb high enough to be safe. There was no escape.

Then the shark broke the surface of the water. It was a bull shark. It opened its mouth, showing a set of **DAGGER-SHARP** teeth.

"JAKE!" screamed his mom.

"¡OLÉ!" shouted Jake. He thrust the laptop at the shark with a mighty heave. The laptop lodged in the shark's mouth and it speared away to one side, missing Jake. It wriggled back and forth.

"Enjoy your feed!" yelled Jake. He reached for the ladder, keeping one eye out for the now-distressed shark. His mom had dragged Mr. Lamb up a couple of rungs. That was all the rungs Jake needed.

CRUNCH! The bull shark chewed through the laptop's casing. The casing splintered and sparks SIZZLED and FLASHED. The shark forgot all about Jake and rushed back to the tunnel. Jake scrambled onto the ladder.

With a few shoves from Jake and some heaves from his mom, they edged Mr. Lamb up the ladder to safety.

Jake collapsed into his mom's arms. "I'll never say a bad thing about computers ever again!" he said.

Jake woke up, blinking. Sunshine was streaming in through the window. Then he remembered: He was in a guest room at Shark Park; it was morning.

Jake dragged on some clothes and headed toward the cafe. He could hear his mum and Mr. Lamb arguing.

"I take your comments very seriously," said Mr. Lamb.

"I hope you do, Mr. Lamb," said Dr. Edwards. "Because if you don't—"

She paused as Jake entered the room.

"Good morning," said Jake. He flopped down at the table. "That was some **FUN** we had yesterday!" he said.

Mr. Lamb stared at Jake, then broke into laughter. "Yes, indeedy-do!" he chuckled. "That was some fun!"

"How's your ankle?" asked Jake.

Mr. Lamb shrugged. "Much better. Thank you for being such a hero." Then he frowned. "Your mother has been telling me about all of the things I did wrong," he said.

"From today, I will be employing keepers for all my exhib—." He grinned. "Sorry. For all of my *guests*. I will be looking at emergency procedures. I will be feeding my guests **REGULARLY**. And I won't be opening Shark Park to the public until I fix everything that is wrong."

He turned to Jake. "And when I do, I hope that you and your mom will come along for a tour."

"Only if Mom can bring her laptop!" said Jake, grinning.